Sacred Strategies

20 Biblical Principles Branding for Your *Business*

Copyright © 2024 Larry Daniels

Published by: Branding + The Bible

All rights reserved. In accordance with the U.S.

Copyright Act of 1976, no part of this publication may be reproduced in any form or by any means, including scanning, photocopying, or otherwise without prior written permission from the copyright holder.

Published in the United States of America

Language: English

Chapter 1
Authentic Storytelling:
The Power of Testimony

Introduction: Unveiling the Power of Testimony

In the dynamic realm of branding and marketing, the concept of authenticity stands as a beacon, guiding businesses toward meaningful connections with their audience. Authentic storytelling, rooted in personal experiences and genuine emotions, holds the key to unlocking the hearts and minds of consumers. As we embark on this journey, drawing wisdom from the narratives woven throughout the Bible, we illuminate the path toward building compelling brand identities through the power of testimony.

The Story of David: Transparency in Triumph and Tribulation

David, the shepherd-king of Israel, emerges as a towering figure in the annals of biblical history. His narrative resonates with authenticity, marked by both triumphs and tribulations. From his courageous defeat of Goliath to his infamous affair with Bathsheba, David's life unfolds as an open book, revealing the complexities of human nature. Despite his flaws, David's unwavering faith and transparent acknowledgment of his mistakes endear him to his people, cementing his legacy as a man after God's own heart.

In the business world, David's example serves as a poignant reminder of the power of transparency. Entrepreneurs who embrace authenticity, openly acknowledging both their successes and failures, foster trust and credibility with their audience. By sharing personal anecdotes and lessons learned along their entrepreneurial journey, business owners can humanize their brand, forging deeper connections with customers based on mutual understanding and empathy.

The Testimony of Paul: Transformation and Transparency

The apostle Paul's journey from persecutor to preacher embodies the transformative power of authenticity. His encounter with the risen Christ on the road to Damascus marks a pivotal moment in his life, catalyzing a profound internal transformation. Paul's letters to the early Christian communities bear witness to his authenticity, as he candidly shares his struggles and shortcomings while steadfastly proclaiming the gospel message.

Paul's example underscores the importance of vulnerability in storytelling. In the business landscape, entrepreneurs who are willing to embrace vulnerability and share their authentic selves with their audience create opportunities for genuine connection. By weaving personal anecdotes and insights into their brand narrative, business owners can cultivate a sense of intimacy and trust, fostering loyalty and advocacy among their customers.

Application in Business: Crafting Compelling Brand Narratives

As Christian entrepreneurs, we are called to emulate the authenticity displayed by biblical figures like David and Paul in our business endeavors. Authentic storytelling begins with a willingness to share our own stories—our triumphs, setbacks, and moments of transformation. By infusing our brand narrative with authenticity and transparency, we invite customers into a deeper conversation, one that transcends mere transactions and fosters genuine connection.

Practical steps for implementing authentic storytelling in business include:

1. **Know Your Story**: Reflect on your personal journey as an entrepreneur. What challenges have you faced? What lessons have you learned? Identify key moments that have shaped your identity and your brand.

2. **Share Authentically**: Be genuine in your communication with your audience. Share personal anecdotes and insights that highlight your values and beliefs. Avoid the temptation to present a polished facade—authenticity resonates with customers far more than perfection.

3. **Connect Emotionally**: Tap into the power of emotion to forge deeper connections with your audience. Whether through heartfelt testimonials, compelling narratives, or

inspirational messages, strive to evoke genuine emotional responses that resonate with your customers' experiences and aspirations.

4. **Be Consistent**: Authentic storytelling is an ongoing process, not a one-time event. Consistently reinforce your brand narrative across all touchpoints, from your website and social media channels to your marketing materials and customer interactions.

5. **Listen and Adapt**: Pay attention to feedback from your audience and be willing to adapt your storytelling approach accordingly. Authenticity is not static—it evolves as you learn and grow as an entrepreneur.

Conclusion: Harnessing the Power of Authentic Storytelling

In the tapestry of business, authentic storytelling stands as a thread that binds brands to their audience in meaningful ways. Drawing inspiration from the biblical narratives of David and Paul, we uncover timeless principles that illuminate the path toward building compelling brand identities rooted in authenticity and transparency. By infusing our brand narratives with personal testimony, we invite customers into a shared journey—one defined by honesty, empathy, and genuine connection. As we continue our exploration of biblical principles in branding and marketing, may we embrace the transformative power of authenticity, shaping not only our businesses but also the hearts and minds of those we serve.

Chapter 2
Building Community:
The Acts of Fellowship

Introduction: The Power of Community in Business

In the bustling marketplace, businesses often fixate on transactions and profits, sometimes neglecting the vital role of community in fostering sustainable growth and brand loyalty. Just as the early Christian community flourished through fellowship and mutual support, modern businesses can harness the power of community to cultivate a loyal customer base, drive repeat business, and foster brand advocacy. In this chapter, we explore how the timeless principles of community building found within the pages of the Bible can be applied to create vibrant communities of customers who not only purchase products or services but also become brand ambassadors and advocates.

The Acts of Fellowship: Unity in Diversity

The book of Acts paints a vivid picture of the early Christian community, characterized by a deep sense of fellowship and unity. Despite their diverse backgrounds and cultural differences, believers came together as one body, sharing their resources, supporting one another, and spreading the message of hope and redemption. This sense of unity and belonging fostered a vibrant community that transcended geographical boundaries and cultural barriers.

In the realm of business, building a community of customers requires fostering a similar sense of unity and belonging. Businesses must create spaces where customers feel valued, heard, and connected to something greater than a mere transaction. By embracing diversity and inclusivity, businesses can build communities that welcome individuals from all walks of life, fostering a sense of belonging and shared purpose.

Lessons from Acts: Nurturing Relationships and Trust

The early Christian community offers valuable insights into the importance of nurturing relationships and building trust. Acts recounts numerous instances where believers demonstrated unwavering support for one another, whether through acts of kindness, financial assistance, or emotional support. These interactions fostered a deep sense of trust and solidarity among believers, strengthening the bonds of fellowship and unity.

Similarly, in the business world, building a community of customers requires prioritizing relationship-building and trust. Businesses must invest in cultivating meaningful connections with their customers, listening to their needs and concerns, and delivering exceptional experiences that foster loyalty and advocacy. By prioritizing transparency, integrity, and empathy in their interactions, businesses can earn the trust and loyalty of their community, laying the foundation for long-term success.

Application in Business: Cultivating a Community of Customers

As Christian entrepreneurs, we are called to emulate the spirit of fellowship and unity exemplified by the early Christian community in our businesses. Building a community of customers begins with fostering a culture of connection and belonging, where individuals feel valued, heard, and empowered to contribute to the success of the brand. Here are some practical steps for cultivating a community of customers:

1. **Create Engaging Spaces**: Establish online and offline platforms where customers can connect with one another and with your brand. This could include social media groups, forums, events, or loyalty programs that encourage interaction and participation.

2. **Facilitate Meaningful Conversations**: Foster dialogue and engagement within your community by asking questions, soliciting feedback, and facilitating conversations around topics of interest to your customers. Actively listen to their perspectives and incorporate their input into your business decisions.

3. **Offer Exclusive Benefits**: Reward your community members for their loyalty and advocacy by offering exclusive benefits, discounts, or perks. This could include early access to new products or services, special promotions, or VIP experiences that make them feel valued and appreciated.

4. **Encourage User-Generated Content**: Empower your community members to become brand advocates by encouraging them to share their experiences and stories with others. User-generated content, such as testimonials, reviews, and social media posts, not only strengthens brand credibility but also fosters a sense of ownership and belonging among customers.

5. **Foster a Culture of Gratitude**: Express appreciation and gratitude to your community members for their support and engagement. Whether through personalized thank-you notes, special acknowledgments, or surprise gifts, show your customers that their contributions are valued and recognized.

Conclusion: Embracing the Power of Customer Community

In conclusion, building a community of customers is not just about driving transactions—it's about fostering meaningful connections and relationships that transcend the confines of commerce. By drawing inspiration from the principles of fellowship and unity found within the pages of the Bible, businesses can create vibrant communities of customers who not only purchase products or services but also become brand advocates and ambassadors. As Christian entrepreneurs, let us continue to build businesses that not only succeed financially but also enrich the lives of those we serve, fostering a spirit of fellowship and unity that transforms customers into loyal advocates and friends.

Chapter 3
Creative Innovation:
Learning from Jesus' Ministry

Introduction: Unveiling the Creative Genius of Jesus

When we think of Jesus' ministry, we often focus on his teachings and miracles. However, beneath the surface lies a profound creativity that shaped his approach to spreading the message of hope and redemption. In this chapter, we delve into the innovative strategies employed by Jesus in his ministry and explore how we can harness creativity to elevate our brand and marketing efforts.

The Creative Ministry of Jesus: Thinking Outside the Box

Jesus' ministry was marked by innovative approaches that challenged conventional norms and captivated audiences. From his use of parables to his unconventional methods of healing, Jesus demonstrated a keen understanding of human psychology and communication. He met people where they were, using relatable stories and vivid imagery to convey timeless truths in ways that resonated deeply with his listeners.

In the business world, creativity is a powerful tool for capturing attention, fostering engagement, and inspiring action. Like Jesus, entrepreneurs can think outside the box, experimenting with novel ideas and approaches to stand out in a crowded marketplace. By tapping into their creative potential, businesses can create memorable brand experiences that leave a lasting impression on customers.

Lessons from Jesus' Creativity: Embracing Innovation and Adaptation

Jesus' creative ministry offers valuable lessons for entrepreneurs seeking to innovate and adapt in today's rapidly changing business landscape. He was not bound by tradition or convention but instead embraced innovation as a means of reaching hearts and minds. Jesus was adaptable, tailoring his message and methods to suit the needs and preferences of his audience, whether preaching to crowds or engaging in one-on-one interactions.

Similarly, in the realm of branding and marketing, entrepreneurs must embrace innovation and adaptability to stay relevant and competitive. By continually seeking new ways to connect with their target audience, businesses can remain at the forefront of industry trends and consumer preferences. Whether through cutting-edge technology, experiential marketing, or creative storytelling, entrepreneurs can leverage creativity to differentiate their brand and drive growth.

Application in Brand and Marketing: Unleashing Your Creative Potential

As Christian entrepreneurs, we are called to emulate the creative genius of Jesus in our brand and marketing efforts. Creativity begins with a willingness to challenge the status quo and explore new possibilities. Here are some practical steps for unleashing your creative potential:

1. **Understand Your Audience**: Take the time to understand your target audience—their needs, desires, and pain points. By gaining insight into their preferences and behaviors, you can tailor your brand and marketing strategies to resonate with them on a deeper level.

2. **Tell Compelling Stories**: Embrace the power of storytelling to capture the imagination of your audience and create emotional connections with your brand. Draw inspiration from Jesus' use of parables, crafting narratives that communicate your brand's values and vision in a memorable and engaging way.

3. **Experiment and Iterate**: Don't be afraid to experiment with new ideas and approaches in your branding and marketing efforts. Test different strategies, measure their effectiveness, and iterate based on feedback and results. Embrace failure as a learning opportunity and remain open to pivoting when necessary.

4. **Embrace Technology**: Leverage technology to enhance your brand and marketing initiatives. From social media platforms to augmented reality experiences, embrace

innovative tools and technologies that enable you to connect with your audience in unique and meaningful ways.

5. **Collaborate and Innovate**: Foster a culture of collaboration and innovation within your organization, encouraging employees to share their ideas and contribute to the creative process. By tapping into the diverse perspectives and talents of your team, you can unlock new opportunities for growth and differentiation.

Conclusion: Embracing Creativity as a Catalyst for Growth

In conclusion, the creative genius of Jesus offers a powerful example for entrepreneurs seeking to elevate their brand and marketing efforts. By embracing innovation, adaptation, and creativity, businesses can create memorable brand experiences that resonate with their audience and drive growth. As Christian entrepreneurs, let us draw inspiration from Jesus' ministry, thinking outside the box and unleashing our creative potential to make a lasting impact on the world around us. In doing so, we not only honor the legacy of Jesus' creativity but also pave the way for transformative growth and success in our businesses.

Chapter 4
Value Proposition:
Unveiling the Hidden Treasure

Introduction: Understanding the Power of Value Proposition

In the competitive landscape of business, defining and communicating a compelling value proposition is essential for capturing the attention and loyalty of customers. Just as the hidden treasure in Jesus' parable held immense value, a well-crafted value proposition distinguishes a brand from its competitors and communicates the unique benefits it offers to customers. In this chapter, we explore the timeless wisdom of uncovering and showcasing the hidden treasures within your brand, drawing inspiration from biblical principles and practical insights.

The Parable of the Hidden Treasure: Discovering Unparalleled Value

In the parable of the hidden treasure, Jesus illustrates the concept of value proposition through a powerful metaphor. A man stumbles upon a hidden treasure buried in a field and, recognizing its immense value, sells all he has to acquire the field. This story highlights the transformative power of discovering something of extraordinary worth and the sacrifices one is willing to make to obtain it.

Similarly, in business, a value proposition serves as the cornerstone of a brand's identity, encapsulating the unique benefits and advantages it offers to customers. By uncovering the hidden treasures within your brand—whether it's exceptional quality, innovative solutions, or unparalleled customer service—you can differentiate yourself from competitors and attract customers who recognize and appreciate your value.

Crafting a Compelling Value Proposition: Communicating Your Brand's Unique Benefits

Crafting a compelling value proposition begins with a deep understanding of your target audience and their needs, desires, and pain points. By identifying the specific problems your product or service solves and the benefits it delivers, you can create a value proposition that resonates with customers on an emotional and practical level.

Incorporate the following elements into your value proposition:

1. **Identify Customer Pain Points**: Understand the challenges and frustrations your target audience faces and position your brand as the solution to their problems.

2. **Highlight Unique Benefits**: Clearly communicate the unique benefits and advantages your product or service offers that set you apart from competitors.

3. **Emphasize Value**: Quantify the value customers receive from choosing your brand, whether it's cost savings, time efficiency, or improved quality of life.

4. **Be Clear and Concise**: Keep your value proposition clear, concise, and easy to understand, avoiding jargon or technical language that may confuse or alienate customers.

Application in Business: Elevating Your Brand with a Compelling Value Proposition

As Christian entrepreneurs, we are called to emulate the wisdom of the hidden treasure parable in our branding and marketing efforts. By uncovering the unique treasures within our brand and communicating them effectively to customers, we can differentiate ourselves in the marketplace and attract a loyal following. Here are some practical steps for crafting and communicating a compelling value proposition:

1. **Conduct Market Research**: Invest time in understanding your target audience and their needs, preferences, and pain points through market research, surveys, and customer feedback.

2. **Identify Unique Selling Points**: Identify the unique features, benefits, or qualities that set your brand apart from competitors and resonate with your target audience.

3. **Define Your Value Proposition**: Articulate your brand's value proposition in a clear, concise statement that communicates the specific benefits customers will receive from choosing your brand.

4. **Integrate Your Value Proposition**: Incorporate your value proposition into all aspects of your branding and marketing efforts, including your website, advertising campaigns, social media presence, and customer communications.

5. **Test and Iterate**: Continuously monitor and evaluate the effectiveness of your value proposition, soliciting feedback from customers and making adjustments as needed to ensure it remains relevant and compelling.

Conclusion: Unveiling the Hidden Treasures Within Your Brand

In conclusion, the parable of the hidden treasure serves as a powerful metaphor for the concept of value proposition in business. By uncovering the unique treasures within your brand and communicating them effectively to customers, you can differentiate yourself in the marketplace and attract a loyal following. As Christian entrepreneurs, let us draw inspiration from this timeless wisdom, crafting value propositions that resonate with customers on both practical and emotional levels. In doing so, we not only elevate our brands but also fulfill our calling to serve others and make a positive impact in the world.

Chapter 5
Consistent Branding:

Introduction: The Eternal Wisdom of Consistent Branding

In the ever-changing landscape of business, consistency in branding stands as a timeless principle rooted in the pages of Scripture. Just as God remains steadfast and unchanging, businesses can harness the power of consistent branding to build trust and loyalty among customers. In this chapter, we'll explore how biblical principles provide a blueprint for achieving consistency in branding and how they can be applied in business today.

The Biblical Foundation of Consistent Branding

Consistent branding finds its roots in the unchanging truths of Scripture, offering invaluable insights for modern businesses:

Visual Identity: Reflecting God's Immutable Nature

Just as God's character remains unwavering, businesses can emulate consistency in their visual identity. The Bible assures us of God's steadfastness in Psalm 102:27: "But you remain the same, and your years will never end." By maintaining consistency in logos, colors, and imagery, businesses mirror God's unchanging nature and cultivate trust among customers.

Messaging: Communicating Truth with Integrity

Proverbs 12:22 reminds us, "The Lord detests lying lips, but he delights in people who are trustworthy." Similarly, consistent messaging reflects integrity and truthfulness, aligning with God's character. By upholding a consistent brand voice and messaging style, businesses convey authenticity and reliability to their audience.

Tone: Speaking with Grace and Consistency

Colossians 4:6 advises, "Let your conversation be always full of grace, seasoned with salt, so that you may know how to answer everyone." Consistent tone in brand communications reflects grace and humility, mirroring the gentle and steadfast nature of Christ. By maintaining a consistent tone across all interactions, businesses embody the principles of grace and reliability.

Customer Experience: Serving with Compassion and Excellence

Ephesians 6:7 reminds us, "Serve wholeheartedly, as if you were serving the Lord, not people." Consistent delivery of products and services reflects a commitment to excellence and compassion, mirroring Christ's servant-hearted leadership. By providing a consistent and reliable customer experience, businesses demonstrate their dedication to serving others with excellence.

Lessons from Scripture: The Power of Consistency

Scripture offers countless examples of consistency and reliability, providing valuable lessons for businesses:

Noah exhibited unwavering faithfulness in building the ark according to God's instructions, demonstrating the power of consistency in fulfilling God's purpose (Genesis 6:22).

The Israelites relied on God's provision of manna in the wilderness, experiencing the faithfulness of His provision day after day (Exodus 16:35).

Jesus Christ, the same yesterday, today, and forever, exemplifies the ultimate consistency in character and purpose (Hebrews 13:8).

Application in Business: Implementing Biblical Consistency Strategies

Christian entrepreneurs can apply biblical principles to achieve consistent branding in their businesses:

Establish Brand Guidelines Rooted in Truth: Develop comprehensive brand guidelines that reflect biblical values of integrity and authenticity.

Embrace God's Design in Design: Infuse design elements with biblical symbolism and imagery, reflecting the eternal truths found in Scripture.

Communicate with Grace and Clarity: Maintain a consistent brand voice that reflects the grace and truth of Christ in all communications.

Serve with Excellence and Compassion: Prioritize the delivery of products and services that honor God and serve others with excellence and compassion.

Conclusion: Building Trust through Biblical Consistency

In conclusion, consistent branding rooted in biblical principles is essential for building trust and loyalty among customers. By aligning visual identity, messaging, tone, and customer experience with the timeless truths of Scripture, businesses can create a unified brand identity that reflects God's character and fosters long-term relationships. As Christian entrepreneurs, let us strive to uphold principles of integrity and reliability in our branding efforts, reflecting our commitment to excellence and authenticity in all aspects of our business. In doing so, we not only strengthen our brands but also bear witness to God's faithfulness and grace in the marketplace.

Chapter 6
Adaptability:
Thriving in a Changing Landscape

Introduction: The Essence of Adaptability

In the dynamic and ever-evolving world of business, adaptability is not just a trait—it's a necessity for survival and success. The ability to pivot, innovate, and thrive in the face of change distinguishes resilient businesses from those that falter. In this chapter, we delve into the importance of adaptability and explore how it enables businesses to navigate uncertainty and seize opportunities for growth.

The Imperative of Adaptability in Business

Adaptability is rooted in the recognition that change is inevitable and constant. In the natural world, species that adapt to shifting environments survive and thrive, while those that fail to adapt risk extinction. Similarly, in the business world, companies that embrace adaptability are better equipped to withstand disruptions, capitalize on emerging trends, and maintain a competitive edge.

Lessons from Nature: The Survival of the Fittest

Nature offers valuable lessons in adaptability, as organisms evolve to thrive in diverse and often challenging environments. Darwin's theory of natural selection highlights the importance of adaptability in the survival of species. Those that can adapt to changes in their environment, whether through physical traits or behavioral strategies, are more likely to survive and pass on their genes to future generations.

Application in Business: Embracing a Culture of Adaptability

As Christian entrepreneurs, we are called to embrace a culture of adaptability in our businesses, recognizing that change presents opportunities for growth and innovation. Here are some practical strategies for fostering adaptability within your organization:

1. **Cultivate a Growth Mindset**: Encourage employees to adopt a growth mindset, embracing challenges as opportunities for learning and development. Foster a culture where experimentation and failure are viewed as necessary steps on the path to success.

2. **Stay Agile and Flexible**: Structure your organization to be agile and flexible, allowing for rapid response and adaptation to changing market conditions. Empower employees at all levels to make decisions and take initiative in response to emerging opportunities or challenges.

3. **Embrace Innovation**: Foster a culture of innovation that encourages employees to think creatively and explore new

ideas. Provide resources and support for experimentation and prototyping, and celebrate successes and learnings from failures.

4. **Stay Customer-Centric**: Prioritize the needs and preferences of your customers, and be responsive to feedback and changing market trends. Adapt your products, services, and business strategies to meet evolving customer expectations and preferences.

5. **Monitor Trends and Anticipate Change**: Stay informed about industry trends, technological advancements, and macroeconomic factors that may impact your business. Proactively anticipate changes in the competitive landscape and adjust your strategy accordingly.

Conclusion: Navigating Change with Confidence

In conclusion, adaptability is a cornerstone of success in the modern business landscape. By embracing change with resilience and innovation, businesses can navigate uncertainty with confidence and seize opportunities for growth. As Christian entrepreneurs, let us draw inspiration from the lessons of nature and cultivate a culture of adaptability within our organizations. By staying agile, innovative, and customer-centric, we can thrive in a changing world, fulfilling our mission to serve others and make a positive impact in our communities and beyond.

Chapter 7
Innovative Problem-Solving:
Unleashing Creative Solutions

Introduction: The Power of Innovative Problem-Solving

In the journey of business, encountering obstacles and challenges is inevitable. However, it's not the hurdles themselves but our responses to them that shape our success. Innovative problem-solving empowers businesses to navigate adversity creatively, uncovering unique solutions and opportunities for growth. Rooted in biblical wisdom exemplified by King Solomon, this chapter explores the importance of innovative problem-solving and how it enables businesses to overcome obstacles with faith-driven creativity.

The Essence of Innovative Problem-Solving

Innovative problem-solving embodies the spirit of creativity, resilience, and wisdom, traits epitomized by King Solomon in the Bible. Instead of relying solely on conventional wisdom or repeating past strategies, innovative problem-solvers draw inspiration from Solomon's example to approach challenges with fresh perspectives. By embracing experimentation, lateral thinking, and a reliance on divine guidance, businesses can uncover novel solutions that drive progress and honor God's provision.

Lessons from King Solomon: The Art of Creative Thinking

King Solomon, renowned for his wisdom, demonstrated innovative problem-solving in various aspects of his reign. His famous judgment in the case of the two women claiming motherhood of the same child showcases Solomon's astute wisdom and creative approach to resolving disputes. Solomon's dedication to seeking divine wisdom, challenging assumptions, and making bold decisions serves as a timeless example for businesses navigating challenges with faith-driven innovation.

Application in Business: Cultivating a Culture of Innovation

As Christian entrepreneurs, we are called to cultivate a culture of innovation that reflects biblical principles of stewardship, creativity, and reliance on divine guidance, following King Solomon's example. Here are practical strategies for fostering innovative problem-solving within your organization:

1. **Seek Divine Wisdom**: Start by seeking divine wisdom through prayer, meditation on scripture, and discernment, just as Solomon did. Invite God into your decision-making process and trust in His guidance to illuminate creative solutions to your business challenges.

2. **Encourage Creative Thinking**: Create a workplace culture that values and encourages creative thinking. Provide opportunities for brainstorming, ideation, and collaboration, and celebrate innovative ideas that align with your business's mission and values.

3. **Embrace Risk-Taking**: Encourage calculated risk-taking and experimentation as part of your innovation strategy. Embrace the mindset that failure is an opportunity for growth and learning, and celebrate both successes and learnings from setbacks.

4. **Foster Collaboration**: Cultivate a collaborative environment where diverse perspectives are welcomed and respected. Encourage cross-functional teamwork and interdisciplinary collaboration to spark creativity and innovation.

5. **Lead by Example**: As a leader, lead by example by embodying the principles of innovative problem-solving in your own actions and decision-making. Demonstrate humility, resilience, and a willingness to embrace change as you navigate challenges and pursue opportunities for growth, following in the footsteps of King Solomon.

Conclusion: Driving Progress through Faith-Driven Innovation

In conclusion, innovative problem-solving is not just a strategic approach—it's a reflection of our faith in God's provision and guidance, exemplified by King Solomon's wisdom. By drawing inspiration from biblical principles and embracing creativity, resilience, and divine wisdom, businesses can navigate obstacles with confidence and uncover new pathways to success. As Christian entrepreneurs, let us cultivate a culture of innovation rooted in faith, stewardship, and a relentless pursuit of God's purpose for our businesses. In doing so, we honor God's provision, drive progress, and make a positive impact in the world.

Chapter 8
Strategic Partnerships:
The Friendship of David and Jonathan

Introduction: The Power of Strategic Partnerships

In the world of business, strategic partnerships can be transformative, opening doors to new opportunities, resources, and markets. Just as the friendship between David and Jonathan in the Bible proved to be strategically significant, so too can strategic partnerships propel businesses forward in pursuit of shared goals and mutual success. In this chapter, we explore the timeless wisdom of the friendship between David and Jonathan and its relevance for cultivating strategic partnerships in business.

The Story of David and Jonathan: A Model of Strategic Friendship

The biblical account of David and Jonathan's friendship is a testament to the power of strategic alliances. Despite the political and familial tensions surrounding their relationship, David and Jonathan forged a deep bond based on mutual respect, trust, and shared values. Jonathan recognized David's leadership potential and selflessly supported him, even at great personal cost, laying the foundation for a strategic partnership that would shape the course of Israel's history.

Key Principles of Strategic Partnerships

The friendship between David and Jonathan offers valuable insights into the principles of effective strategic partnerships:

1. **Mutual Respect and Trust**: David and Jonathan's friendship was built on a foundation of mutual respect and trust. They honored each other's strengths and supported one another through adversity, fostering a sense of loyalty and camaraderie that transcended personal interests.

2. **Shared Values and Goals**: Despite their differences in status and circumstances, David and Jonathan shared common values and goals. Their alignment around the greater good of Israel's well-being enabled them to collaborate effectively and pursue shared objectives with unity of purpose.

3. **Complementary Skills and Resources**: David and Jonathan brought complementary skills and resources to their partnership. Jonathan's military prowess and strategic acumen complemented David's leadership and courage on the battlefield, creating a synergistic partnership that maximized their collective impact.

4. **Commitment to Collaboration**: David and Jonathan were committed to collaboration, recognizing that they could achieve more together than they could alone. They leveraged their respective networks and influence to support each

other's endeavors, fostering a spirit of cooperation and mutual benefit.

Application in Business: Cultivating Strategic Partnerships

Drawing inspiration from the friendship of David and Jonathan, businesses can cultivate strategic partnerships that drive growth and innovation. Here are practical steps for fostering strategic partnerships in business:

1. **Identify Shared Values and Goals**: Seek out partners who share your organization's values and goals, aligning around a common purpose that provides a strong foundation for collaboration.

2. **Build Trust and Rapport**: Invest time and effort in building trust and rapport with potential partners, demonstrating integrity, transparency, and reliability in your interactions.

3. **Assess Complementary Skills and Resources**: Evaluate potential partners based on their complementary skills, resources, and networks that can enhance your organization's capabilities and reach.

4. **Establish Clear Expectations**: Define roles, responsibilities, and expectations upfront to ensure clarity and alignment among partners. Establish clear

communication channels and mechanisms for resolving conflicts or addressing challenges that may arise.

5. **Nurture Long-Term Relationships**: Cultivate long-term relationships with strategic partners based on mutual respect, trust, and ongoing collaboration. Regularly communicate and evaluate the partnership's progress, identifying opportunities for growth and innovation together.

Conclusion: The Strategic Imperative of Partnership

In conclusion, the friendship of David and Jonathan offers a timeless example of the strategic importance of partnerships. By cultivating relationships based on mutual respect, trust, and shared goals, businesses can unlock new opportunities, resources, and markets that drive growth and innovation. As Christian entrepreneurs, let us draw inspiration from the principles of strategic partnership exemplified by David and Jonathan, forging alliances that advance our collective mission and impact in the world. In doing so, we honor God's call to stewardship and collaboration, leveraging our talents and resources for the greater good.

Chapter 9
Effective Communication:
The Sermon on the Mount

Introduction: The Importance of Effective Communication

In the realm of business, effective communication is the cornerstone of success, facilitating understanding, collaboration, and alignment among stakeholders. Just as Jesus' Sermon on the Mount captivated and inspired crowds, so too can effective communication captivate and inspire employees, customers, and partners in the business world. In this chapter, we explore the timeless wisdom of the Sermon on the Mount and its relevance for cultivating effective communication in business.

The Sermon on the Mount: A Masterclass in Communication

The Sermon on the Mount, delivered by Jesus to a large crowd gathered on a mountainside, is one of the most renowned speeches in history. In this sermon, Jesus communicated profound truths with clarity, simplicity, and authority, captivating the hearts and minds of his listeners. His message of love, compassion, and righteousness resonated deeply with the crowd, transcending cultural and societal barriers.

Key Principles of Effective Communication

The Sermon on the Mount offers valuable insights into the principles of effective communication:

1. **Clarity and Simplicity**: Jesus communicated complex spiritual truths in a clear and simple manner that resonated with his audience. His use of parables, analogies, and vivid imagery made abstract concepts accessible and relatable, ensuring that his message was understood by people from all walks of life.

2. **Authenticity and Transparency**: Jesus spoke with authenticity and transparency, expressing genuine compassion and empathy for the struggles and challenges faced by his audience. His sincerity and vulnerability fostered trust and credibility, creating a connection with his listeners that transcended mere words.

3. **Empathy and Understanding**: Jesus demonstrated empathy and understanding towards his audience, addressing their needs, fears, and aspirations with compassion and grace. His ability to empathize with the human condition allowed him to connect with people on a deeply personal level, fostering a sense of solidarity and mutual respect.

4. **Inspiration and Motivation**: Jesus' words were not only informative but also inspirational, stirring hearts and minds to action. His message of love, forgiveness, and redemption

inspired his followers to strive for righteousness and pursue a higher purpose in life, igniting a spark of hope and transformation within them.

Application in Business: Cultivating Effective Communication

Drawing inspiration from the Sermon on the Mount, businesses can cultivate effective communication practices that foster understanding, collaboration, and alignment. Here are practical steps for cultivating effective communication in business:

1. **Clarity and Conciseness**: Communicate with clarity and conciseness, avoiding jargon and unnecessary complexity. Use simple language and clear messaging to ensure that your audience understands and retains key information.

2. **Authenticity and Transparency**: Communicate with authenticity and transparency, speaking from the heart and sharing genuine insights and experiences. Build trust and credibility with your audience by being honest, open, and vulnerable in your communications.

3. **Empathy and Active Listening**: Practice empathy and active listening in your communications, seeking to understand the perspectives, concerns, and needs of your audience. Show genuine interest in their experiences and emotions, and respond with compassion and understanding.

4. **Inspiration and Motivation**: Inspire and motivate your audience through your communications, sharing stories, examples, and insights that resonate with their values and aspirations. Paint a compelling vision of the future and empower your audience to take action towards realizing it.

Conclusion: The Transformative Power of Communication

In conclusion, effective communication is essential for fostering understanding, collaboration, and alignment in business. By drawing inspiration from the Sermon on the Mount and applying its principles of clarity, authenticity, empathy, and inspiration, businesses can cultivate communication practices that resonate with their audience and drive positive change. As Christian entrepreneurs, let us strive to communicate with the same clarity, compassion, and conviction as Jesus, inspiring others to embrace our shared vision and values. In doing so, we honor God's call to stewardship and service, using our words to uplift, empower, and transform lives.

Chapter 10
Emotional Branding:
The Compassion of Jesus

Introduction: The Power of Emotional Branding

In the realm of business, emotional branding holds the key to building deep, lasting connections with customers. Just as Jesus' compassion touched the hearts of those he encountered, so too can businesses evoke powerful emotions that resonate with their audience. In this chapter, we explore the profound impact of emotional branding and draw inspiration from the compassion of Jesus to guide our approach.

The Compassion of Jesus: A Model for Emotional Branding

Jesus' ministry was characterized by compassion—compassion for the sick, the marginalized, and the brokenhearted. His genuine empathy and care for others transcended societal norms and touched the deepest recesses of the human soul. The stories of Jesus healing the sick, feeding the hungry, and comforting the grieving serve as powerful examples of emotional branding in action.

Key Principles of Emotional Branding

The compassion of Jesus offers valuable insights into the principles of emotional branding:

1. **Empathy and Understanding**: Jesus demonstrated empathy and understanding towards those he encountered, meeting them at their point of need and offering comfort and healing. Similarly, businesses can cultivate empathy for their customers' experiences, seeking to understand their desires, fears, and aspirations.

2. **Authenticity and Vulnerability**: Jesus' compassion was authentic and vulnerable, reflecting genuine care and concern for others. In the same way, businesses can build emotional connections with their audience by being authentic and transparent in their communications and actions.

3. **Connection and Community**: Jesus' compassion fostered a sense of connection and community among his followers, uniting them in a shared mission of love and service. Likewise, businesses can create emotional bonds with their customers by fostering a sense of belonging and community around their brand.

4. **Transformation and Hope**: Jesus' compassion brought about transformation and hope in the lives of those he touched, offering a glimpse of a better future. Similarly, businesses can inspire hope and optimism through their brand messaging and experiences, offering solutions that address their customers' needs and aspirations.

Application in Business: Harnessing the Power of Emotional Branding

Drawing inspiration from the compassion of Jesus, businesses can harness the power of emotional branding to build meaningful connections with their audience. Here are practical steps for leveraging emotional branding in business:

1. **Identify Core Values and Mission**: Define your brand's core values and mission, aligning them with principles of compassion, empathy, and service. Communicate these values authentically and consistently across all touchpoints to resonate with your audience.

2. **Tell Compelling Stories**: Share compelling stories that evoke emotion and resonate with your audience's experiences and aspirations. Highlight moments of compassion, kindness, and generosity that reflect your brand's values and mission.

3. **Create Memorable Experiences**: Design memorable experiences that engage the senses and evoke positive emotions. From product design and packaging to customer service interactions, ensure that every touchpoint reinforces your brand's emotional resonance.

4. **Engage with Authenticity**: Interact with your audience authentically and transparently, demonstrating genuine care

and concern for their well-being. Actively listen to their feedback and respond with empathy and understanding.

Conclusion: Building Lasting Connections through Emotional Branding

In conclusion, emotional branding offers businesses a powerful tool for building lasting connections with their audience. By drawing inspiration from the compassion of Jesus and applying principles of empathy, authenticity, connection, and transformation, businesses can create meaningful brand experiences that resonate with their customers on a deep emotional level. As Christian entrepreneurs, let us strive to infuse our brands with the same compassion and empathy that Jesus demonstrated, creating positive impact and fostering transformation in the lives of those we serve. In doing so, we honor God's call to love and serve others, using our businesses as vehicles for compassion and healing in the world.

Chapter 11
Differentiation:
The Calling of Abraham

Introduction: The Significance of Differentiation

In the competitive landscape of business, differentiation is crucial for standing out amidst the crowd and capturing the attention of customers. Just as Abraham's calling set him apart as a distinct and chosen leader, businesses can differentiate themselves by embracing their unique identity, values, and offerings. In this chapter, we explore the timeless wisdom of Abraham's calling and its relevance for differentiating businesses in today's market.

The Calling of Abraham: A Blueprint for Differentiation

Abraham's calling by God marked the beginning of a journey that would set him apart as a distinct leader and patriarch. God's promise to bless him and make him a great nation distinguished Abraham from his contemporaries, positioning him as a chosen vessel for God's purposes. Abraham's obedience, faith, and willingness to embrace his unique calling laid the foundation for a legacy that continues to inspire generations.

Key Principles of Differentiation

The calling of Abraham offers valuable insights into the principles of differentiation:

1.**Clarity of Purpose**: Abraham's calling provided him with a clear sense of purpose and direction, setting him apart as a leader with a unique mission to fulfill. Similarly, businesses can differentiate themselves by defining a clear purpose and vision that resonates with their audience and distinguishes them from competitors.

2.**Distinctive Identity**: Abraham's identity as the father of many nations set him apart as a distinct and influential figure in history. Likewise, businesses can differentiate themselves by embracing their unique identity, values, and culture, reflecting authenticity and integrity in all aspects of their operations.

3. **Bold Innovation**: Abraham's willingness to step out in faith and embrace the unknown demonstrated a spirit of bold innovation and risk-taking. Similarly, businesses can differentiate themselves by embracing innovation and creativity, challenging the status quo, and pioneering new solutions that address unmet needs in the market.

4.**Commitment to Excellence**: Abraham's commitment to excellence and integrity in fulfilling his calling earned him respect and admiration from those around him. Likewise, businesses can differentiate themselves by delivering exceptional quality, value, and service that exceed customer expectations and foster long-term loyalty.

Application in Business: Embracing Differentiation

Drawing inspiration from the calling of Abraham, businesses can embrace differentiation to stand out in today's competitive market. Here are practical steps for leveraging differentiation in business:

1.**Define Your Unique Value Proposition**: Identify and articulate your unique value proposition that sets your business apart from competitors. Clearly communicate what makes your brand special and why customers should choose you over alternatives.

2.**Embrace Your Authentic Identity**: Embrace your authentic identity, values, and culture as the foundation of your differentiation strategy. Ensure that your brand personality shines through in all aspects of your marketing, messaging, and customer interactions.

3. **Innovate with Purpose**: Innovate with purpose, focusing on solutions that address unmet needs and add value to your customers' lives. Be willing to take calculated risks and explore new opportunities for growth and differentiation.

4. **Deliver Consistent Excellence**: Commit to delivering consistent excellence in all aspects of your business, from product quality and customer service to marketing and branding. Strive to exceed customer expectations at every touchpoint and build a reputation for reliability and trustworthiness.

Conclusion: Setting Yourself Apart through Differentiation

In conclusion, differentiation is essential for standing out in today's competitive business landscape. By drawing inspiration from the calling of Abraham and embracing principles of clarity of purpose, distinctive identity, bold innovation, and commitment to excellence, businesses can set themselves apart and capture the attention of customers. As Christian entrepreneurs, let us embrace our unique calling and identity, leveraging differentiation as a means of fulfilling our mission and making a positive impact in the world. In doing so, we honor God's purpose for our businesses and contribute to the flourishing of society.

Chapter 12
Strategic Planning:
The Building of Noah's Ark

Introduction: The Essence of Strategic Planning

In the realm of business, strategic planning lays the groundwork for success, guiding organizations through uncertainty and complexity toward their desired goals. Just as Noah meticulously planned and executed the construction of the ark, businesses can leverage strategic planning to navigate challenges and seize opportunities. In this chapter, we explore the strategic wisdom embodied in the building of Noah's Ark and its relevance for modern business strategy.

The Building of Noah's Ark: A Blueprint for Strategic Planning

Noah's obedience to God's command to build an ark to withstand the impending flood exemplifies strategic planning at its finest. Despite facing skepticism and ridicule from his contemporaries, Noah diligently followed God's instructions, meticulously planning every aspect of the ark's design, construction, and provisioning. His foresight, discipline, and commitment to the task ensured the survival of his family and the preservation of countless species.

Key Principles of Strategic Planning

The building of Noah's Ark offers valuable insights into the principles of strategic planning:

1. **Vision and Purpose**: Noah's vision to build the ark was driven by a clear sense of purpose—to obey God's command and preserve life amidst impending destruction. Similarly, businesses must articulate a compelling vision and purpose that guides their strategic planning efforts and inspires stakeholders to action.

2. **Risk Management and Contingency Planning:** Noah's strategic planning involved careful risk management and contingency planning to mitigate potential threats and uncertainties. He anticipated challenges such as the duration of the flood and the need to sustain life onboard, taking proactive measures to address them through meticulous planning and preparation.

3. **Resource Allocation and Optimization**: Noah's strategic planning also encompassed resource allocation and optimization, ensuring that he had the necessary materials, manpower, and provisions to complete the ark's construction and sustain its occupants throughout the flood. He leveraged his resources wisely, maximizing efficiency and effectiveness in achieving his objectives.

4. **Adaptability and Flexibility**: Despite the meticulous planning, Noah remained adaptable and flexible in response

to changing circumstances and unforeseen challenges. He demonstrated resilience and resourcefulness, making adjustments to his plans as needed to overcome obstacles and achieve his ultimate goal of preserving life.

Application in Business: Implementing Strategic Planning

Drawing inspiration from the building of Noah's Ark, businesses can implement strategic planning practices that foster resilience, agility, and success. Here are practical steps for leveraging strategic planning in business:

1.**Define Your Vision and Objectives**: Clearly define your organization's vision, mission, and objectives, articulating where you want to go and what you aim to achieve. Ensure alignment among stakeholders and communicate the vision effectively throughout the organization.

2. **Conduct a SWOT Analysis**: Assess your organization's strengths, weaknesses, opportunities, and threats through a SWOT analysis. Identify internal and external factors that may impact your business and use insights from the analysis to inform your strategic planning decisions.

3. **Develop Actionable Strategies**: Develop actionable strategies and initiatives to achieve your organizational objectives, considering factors such as market trends, competitive dynamics, and stakeholder expectations. Set

clear goals, milestones, and performance metrics to track progress and measure success.

4. **Allocate Resources Wisely**: Allocate resources—including finances, manpower, and technology—wisely to support your strategic initiatives. Prioritize investments that align with your strategic priorities and have the greatest potential to drive growth and innovation.

5. **Monitor and Adjust**: Continuously monitor market dynamics, performance metrics, and external factors that may impact your business. Remain adaptable and flexible, making adjustments to your strategic plans as needed to capitalize on emerging opportunities or mitigate risks.

Conclusion: Navigating the Waters of Business with Strategic Planning

In conclusion, strategic planning is essential for guiding businesses through uncertainty and complexity toward their desired objectives. By drawing inspiration from the building of Noah's Ark and embracing principles of vision, risk management, resource allocation, and adaptability, businesses can navigate the waters of business with confidence and resilience. As Christian entrepreneurs, let us approach strategic planning with diligence, faith, and foresight, trusting in God's guidance as we chart a course for success. In doing so, we honor God's call to stewardship and excellence, using our businesses as vessels for His purposes in the world.

Chapter 13
Purpose-Driven Branding:
The Mission of Jesus

Introduction: Embracing Purpose-Driven Branding

In today's competitive business landscape, purpose-driven branding has emerged as a powerful strategy for connecting with customers and making a positive impact in the world. Just as Jesus' mission on Earth was driven by a clear sense of purpose, businesses can leverage purpose-driven branding to articulate their mission, values, and impact. In this chapter, we explore the profound significance of Jesus' mission and its relevance for purpose-driven branding in business.

The Mission of Jesus: A Model for Purpose-Driven Branding

Jesus' mission on Earth was centered around proclaiming the Kingdom of God, reconciling humanity to God, and demonstrating God's love and compassion for all people. His unwavering commitment to this mission shaped every aspect of his ministry, from his teachings and miracles to his sacrificial death and resurrection. Jesus' purpose-driven approach to ministry serves as a timeless model for businesses seeking to align their brand with a higher purpose.

Key Principles of Purpose-Driven Branding

The mission of Jesus offers valuable insights into the principles of purpose-driven branding:

1.**Clarity of Purpose**: Jesus' mission was driven by a clear sense of purpose—to fulfill God's plan for salvation and reconciliation. Similarly, purpose-driven branding requires organizations to articulate a compelling purpose that inspires and motivates stakeholders, guiding their actions and decisions.

2. **Authenticity and Integrity**: Jesus' mission was characterized by authenticity and integrity, reflecting genuine care and compassion for others. Likewise, purpose-driven branding requires organizations to align their actions with their stated purpose, demonstrating sincerity and transparency in all interactions.

3. **Impact and Transformation**: Jesus' mission had a profound impact on individuals and communities, transforming lives and bringing about positive change. Purpose-driven branding aims to make a meaningful impact in the world, addressing societal challenges and improving the lives of stakeholders.

4. **Alignment and Consistency:** Jesus' mission was consistent across all aspects of his ministry, from his teachings and actions to his interactions with others.

Similarly, purpose-driven branding requires organizations to ensure alignment and consistency in their messaging, values, and actions, building trust and credibility with stakeholders.

Application in Business: Embracing Purpose-Driven Branding

Drawing inspiration from the mission of Jesus, businesses can embrace purpose-driven branding to differentiate themselves and make a positive impact in the world. Here are practical steps for implementing purpose-driven branding:

1. **Define Your Brand Purpose**: Clearly define your organization's purpose, articulating why you exist and the impact you aim to make in the world. Ensure that your purpose resonates with stakeholders and provides a compelling reason for them to engage with your brand.

2. **Embed Purpose in Your Brand DNA**: Integrate your purpose into every aspect of your brand, from your mission statement and values to your products, services, and customer experiences. Ensure that your purpose is reflected in all communications and interactions with stakeholders.

3. **Engage Stakeholders Authentically**: Engage with stakeholders authentically, demonstrating genuine care and concern for their well-being. Listen to their feedback and

incorporate their perspectives into your decision-making process, fostering a sense of ownership and belonging.

4. **Measure and Communicate Impact**: Measure and communicate the impact of your purpose-driven initiatives, demonstrating tangible outcomes and achievements. Share stories and testimonials that illustrate the difference your brand is making in the lives of individuals and communities.

Conclusion: Harnessing the Power of Purpose-Driven Branding

In conclusion, purpose-driven branding offers businesses a powerful means of connecting with customers, building trust, and making a positive impact in the world. By drawing inspiration from the mission of Jesus and embracing principles of clarity of purpose, authenticity, impact, and alignment, businesses can differentiate themselves and create meaningful connections with stakeholders. As Christian entrepreneurs, let us embrace purpose-driven branding as a vehicle for advancing God's kingdom and serving others with excellence. In doing so, we honor God's call to stewardship and mission, using our businesses to bring about positive change and transformation in the world.

Chapter 14
Adaptive Innovation:
The Acts of Peter and Cornelius

Introduction: Embracing Adaptive Innovation

Innovation is essential for businesses to thrive in an ever-evolving marketplace. However, innovation alone is not enough; businesses must also be adaptable, ready to pivot and evolve in response to changing circumstances. The Acts of Peter and Cornelius offer valuable lessons in adaptive innovation, demonstrating how individuals and organizations can embrace change and innovate in ways that advance their mission and impact. In this chapter, we explore the transformative power of adaptive innovation and its relevance for businesses today.

The Acts of Peter and Cornelius: An Example of Adaptive Innovation

In the book of Acts, we encounter the story of Peter and Cornelius, two individuals from vastly different backgrounds whose encounter sparks a transformative moment in the early Christian community. As a devout Jewish apostle, Peter initially harbored reservations about interacting with Gentiles like Cornelius. However, through a series of divine interventions and personal revelations, Peter's perspective shifted, leading to a groundbreaking moment of inclusivity and innovation in the early church.

Key Principles of Adaptive Innovation

The Acts of Peter and Cornelius offer valuable insights into the principles of adaptive innovation:

1. **Openness to Change**: Peter's willingness to challenge his preconceived notions and embrace change paved the way for adaptive innovation. Similarly, businesses must cultivate a culture of openness to change, encouraging employees to question assumptions and explore new ideas.

2. **Embrace Diversity and Inclusion**: The encounter between Peter and Cornelius highlights the transformative power of embracing diversity and inclusion. Businesses that value diversity and foster inclusive environments are better equipped to innovate and adapt to the needs of diverse stakeholders.

3. **Flexibility and Agility**: Peter's ability to adapt his approach in response to divine guidance demonstrates the importance of flexibility and agility in innovation. Businesses must be willing to pivot and adjust their strategies in response to changing market dynamics and emerging opportunities.

4. **Collaboration and Partnership**: The partnership between Peter and Cornelius exemplifies the value of collaboration in driving innovation. Businesses that leverage partnerships and collaboration across diverse stakeholders can tap into

new perspectives and resources to fuel innovation and growth.

Application in Business: Fostering Adaptive Innovation

Drawing inspiration from the Acts of Peter and Cornelius, businesses can foster adaptive innovation by embracing change, diversity, flexibility, and collaboration. Here are practical steps for fostering adaptive innovation in business:

1. **Create a Culture of Innovation**: Cultivate a culture that values and rewards innovation, encouraging employees to experiment, take risks, and think creatively. Provide resources and support for innovation initiatives and celebrate successes to reinforce the importance of innovation.

2. **Promote Diversity and Inclusion**: Foster a diverse and inclusive workplace where employees feel valued, respected, and empowered to contribute their unique perspectives and talents. Embrace diversity in hiring, leadership, and decision-making to foster innovation and creativity.

3. **Stay Agile and Responsive**: Stay agile and responsive to changing market dynamics and customer needs. Regularly assess market trends, gather feedback from customers and stakeholders, and adapt your strategies and offerings accordingly to stay ahead of the curve.

4. **Forge Strategic Partnerships**: Collaborate with external partners, including suppliers, customers, and industry peers, to tap into new ideas, resources, and markets. Build strategic alliances that complement your strengths and extend your reach, fostering innovation and growth.

Conclusion: Embracing Innovation in an Ever-Changing World

In conclusion, adaptive innovation is essential for businesses to thrive in an ever-changing world. By drawing inspiration from the Acts of Peter and Cornelius and embracing principles of openness to change, diversity, flexibility, and collaboration, businesses can foster a culture of innovation that drives growth and impact. As Christian entrepreneurs, let us embrace adaptive innovation as a means of advancing God's kingdom and serving others with excellence. In doing so, we honor God's call to stewardship and creativity, using our businesses as platforms for positive change and transformation in the world.

Chapter 15
Brand Evangelism:
The Ministry of the Disciples

Introduction: Unleashing Brand Evangelism

In the world of business, brand evangelism is a powerful force that drives customer loyalty, advocacy, and growth. Just as the disciples passionately spread the message of Jesus' teachings, businesses can inspire brand evangelism by cultivating loyal advocates who champion their products and values. In this chapter, we explore the transformative impact of brand evangelism and draw inspiration from the ministry of the disciples to guide our approach.

The Ministry of the Disciples: A Model for Brand Evangelism

The disciples of Jesus embarked on a mission to spread the Good News to the ends of the earth, fervently sharing their experiences and teachings with others. Their passionate advocacy and unwavering commitment to the message of Jesus inspired countless individuals to become followers and advocates themselves, laying the foundation for the growth and expansion of the early Christian movement.

Key Principles of Brand Evangelism

The ministry of the disciples offers valuable insights into the principles of brand evangelism:

1. **Authenticity and Passion**: The disciples' authenticity and passion for their message were infectious, compelling others to take notice and join their cause. Similarly, brand evangelism thrives on genuine passion and enthusiasm for a product or brand, inspiring others to become advocates and ambassadors.

2. **Relationship Building and Community**: The disciples prioritized relationship building and community engagement in their ministry, fostering deep connections with their followers and creating a sense of belonging and solidarity. Likewise, brand evangelism relies on building strong relationships with customers and cultivating a loyal community of advocates and supporters.

3. **Word-of-Mouth Marketing**: The disciples' reliance on word-of-mouth marketing was central to their strategy for spreading the Good News. They leveraged personal recommendations and testimonials to reach new audiences and persuade others to embrace their message. Similarly, brand evangelism harnesses the power of word-of-mouth marketing to amplify the reach and impact of a brand's message.

4. **Consistency and Authenticity**: The disciples' consistent and authentic representation of Jesus' teachings strengthened their credibility and influence as brand

evangelists. Likewise, businesses must maintain consistency and authenticity in their messaging, values, and actions to build trust and loyalty among their advocates.

Application in Business: Cultivating Brand Evangelism

Drawing inspiration from the ministry of the disciples, businesses can cultivate brand evangelism by fostering authenticity, passion, relationship building, and word-of-mouth marketing. Here are practical steps for cultivating brand evangelism in business:

1. **Build a Compelling Brand Story**: Develop a compelling brand story that resonates with customers' values, aspirations, and experiences. Communicate your brand's purpose and mission authentically, inspiring passion and loyalty among your audience.

2. **Empower Customer Advocates**: Identify and empower customer advocates who are passionate about your brand and willing to share their experiences with others. Provide incentives, rewards, and resources to encourage advocacy and amplify the reach of your message.

3. **Foster Community Engagement:** Create opportunities for community engagement and interaction among your customers, fostering a sense of belonging and camaraderie around your brand. Encourage user-generated content,

reviews, and testimonials to amplify the voices of your advocates.

4. **Deliver Exceptional Customer Experiences**: Prioritize delivering exceptional customer experiences at every touchpoint, exceeding expectations and delighting customers with your products, services, and support. Positive experiences will inspire advocacy and loyalty among your customers.

Conclusion: Inspiring Brand Evangelism

In conclusion, brand evangelism is a powerful force that drives customer loyalty, advocacy, and growth. By drawing inspiration from the ministry of the disciples and embracing principles of authenticity, passion, relationship building, and word-of-mouth marketing, businesses can cultivate a community of loyal advocates who champion their brand and message. As Christian entrepreneurs, let us embrace brand evangelism as a means of sharing our values, mission, and impact with the world. In doing so, we honor God's call to stewardship and service, using our businesses as platforms for spreading goodness and inspiring positive change.

Chapter 16
Brand Identity:
The Identity of Jesus

Introduction: Understanding Brand Identity

In the realm of business, brand identity serves as the cornerstone of a company's reputation and recognition. Just as a brand's identity shapes its perception in the marketplace, the identity of Jesus profoundly influences how he is perceived and understood by believers and non-believers alike. In this chapter, we delve into the essence of brand identity through the lens of Jesus' identity and its enduring significance for individuals and organizations seeking to define their own identity.

The Identity of Jesus: A Divine Manifestation

The identity of Jesus encompasses a multitude of dimensions, each contributing to his unique and compelling brand identity. As the Son of God, Jesus embodies divine attributes such as love, compassion, and righteousness. Simultaneously, he is also fully human, experiencing the joys and sorrows of earthly existence. Jesus' identity is further shaped by his roles as a teacher, healer, savior, and shepherd, each reflecting different facets of his character and mission.

Key Elements of Brand Identity

Jesus' identity offers valuable insights into the key elements of brand identity:

1. **Purpose and Mission**: At the core of Jesus' identity is his purpose and mission—to proclaim the Kingdom of God and reconcile humanity to God. Similarly, businesses must define their purpose and mission, articulating why they exist and the impact they aim to make in the world.

2. **Values and Beliefs**: Jesus' identity is shaped by his values and beliefs, including love, compassion, justice, and forgiveness. Likewise, businesses must identify their core values and beliefs, aligning them with their actions and decisions to build trust and credibility with stakeholders.

3. **Personality and Voice**: Jesus' identity is characterized by a distinct personality and voice, reflecting qualities such as humility, wisdom, and authority. Similarly, businesses must develop a brand personality and voice that resonates with their target audience, guiding their communications and interactions.

4. **Visual and Symbolic Elements:** Jesus' identity is often represented visually through symbols such as the cross, the fish, and the shepherd's staff. Likewise, businesses must develop visual and symbolic elements that reinforce their brand identity, including logos, colors, and imagery.

Application in Business: Defining Brand Identity

Drawing inspiration from the identity of Jesus, businesses can define their own brand identity with clarity and purpose. Here are practical steps for defining brand identity:

1. **Articulate Purpose and Values**: Clearly articulate your organization's purpose and values, defining why you exist and the principles that guide your actions and decisions.

2. **Develop a Brand Personality**: Identify the personality traits that define your brand, such as warmth, sincerity, innovation, or reliability. Ensure consistency in how these traits are expressed across all touchpoints.

3. **Create Visual Brand Elements**: Develop visual brand elements that reflect your brand's identity, including logos, typography, color palettes, and imagery. Ensure that these elements align with your brand's personality and values.

4. **Communicate Your Identity**: Consistently communicate your brand identity through all channels, including marketing materials, website content, social media, and customer interactions. Use your brand voice and visual elements to reinforce your identity and build recognition.

Conclusion: Embodying Brand Identity

In conclusion, brand identity is essential for shaping how businesses are perceived and understood by their audience. By drawing inspiration from the identity of Jesus and embracing principles of purpose, values, personality, and visual elements, businesses can define a brand identity that resonates with their target audience and builds lasting connections. As Christian entrepreneurs, let us strive to embody our brand identity with integrity and authenticity, reflecting the values and mission that define who we are and what we stand for. In doing so, we honor God's call to stewardship and excellence, using our businesses as vehicles for positive impact and transformation in the world.

Chapter 17
Data-Driven Decision Making:
The Council at Jerusalem

Introduction: Harnessing Data for Informed Decisions

In the fast-paced world of business, data has become an invaluable asset for making informed decisions and driving strategic initiatives. Just as the Council at Jerusalem relied on evidence and discernment to address a critical issue facing the early church, businesses can leverage data-driven decision-making to navigate complexities and seize opportunities. In this chapter, we explore the significance of data-driven decision-making through the lens of the Council at Jerusalem and its enduring lessons for modern organizations.

The Council at Jerusalem: An Example of Data-Informed Discernment

The Council at Jerusalem, as recorded in the book of Acts, was convened to address a significant theological and practical issue facing the early church—whether Gentile believers should adhere to Jewish customs, particularly circumcision. The apostles and elders gathered to deliberate on this matter, weighing various perspectives and considering the evidence presented to them. Through prayer, reflection, and discernment, they arrived at a decision that aligned with the guidance of the Holy Spirit and the evidence before them.

Key Principles of Data-Driven Decision Making

The Council at Jerusalem offers valuable insights into the principles of data-driven decision making:

1. **Evidence-Based Analysis**: The apostles and elders based their decision on evidence, considering the experiences and testimonies of those involved in ministry among the Gentiles. Similarly, businesses must gather and analyze data from various sources to inform their decisions, including market research, customer feedback, and performance metrics.

2. **Collaborative Discernment**: The Council at Jerusalem involved collaborative discernment, with multiple stakeholders contributing their perspectives and insights. Likewise, businesses should involve diverse teams in the decision-making process, leveraging their expertise and viewpoints to arrive at well-informed conclusions.

3. **Prayerful Reflection**: The apostles and elders engaged in prayerful reflection throughout the decision-making process, seeking divine guidance and wisdom. Similarly, businesses should cultivate a culture of prayer and reflection, acknowledging the importance of spiritual discernment in data-driven decision making.

4. **Alignment with Mission and Values**: The decision reached by the Council at Jerusalem was aligned with the mission and values of the early church, prioritizing unity, inclusion, and the advancement of the Gospel. Likewise, businesses should ensure that data-driven decisions align with their organizational mission, vision, and values, fostering coherence and integrity in their actions.

Application in Business: Implementing Data-Driven Decision Making

Drawing inspiration from the Council at Jerusalem, businesses can implement data-driven decision-making processes that foster clarity, alignment, and effectiveness. Here are practical steps for implementing data-driven decision making in business:

1. **Define Decision Criteria**: Clearly define the criteria and objectives for each decision, identifying the key metrics and indicators that will inform the decision-making process.

2. **Gather Relevant Data**: Collect and analyze relevant data from internal and external sources, including market trends, customer preferences, competitor analysis, and financial performance.

3. **Engage Stakeholders**: Involve relevant stakeholders in the decision-making process, including executives, managers, employees, and external advisors. Encourage open dialogue

and collaboration to ensure diverse perspectives are considered.

4. **Evaluate Options**: Evaluate various options and scenarios based on the data and evidence gathered, weighing the potential risks, benefits, and implications of each decision.

5. **Pray for Guidance**: Seek divine guidance and wisdom through prayer and reflection, acknowledging the spiritual dimension of decision making and inviting God's presence into the process.

6. **Make Informed Decisions**: Make well-informed decisions based on the evidence, discernment, and alignment with organizational mission and values. Communicate the rationale behind the decisions transparently to stakeholders.

Conclusion: Empowering Decisions with Data and Discernment

In conclusion, data-driven decision making empowers businesses to navigate complexities and seize opportunities with confidence and clarity. By drawing inspiration from the Council at Jerusalem and embracing principles of evidence-based analysis, collaborative discernment, prayerful reflection, and alignment with mission and values, businesses can implement data-driven decision-making processes that drive innovation, growth, and impact. As Christian entrepreneurs, let us integrate data and discernment in our decision-making practices, recognizing the importance of both evidence and spiritual guidance in achieving our mission and stewarding our resources effectively. In doing so, we honor God's call to wisdom and stewardship, using data-driven decision making to advance His purposes in the world.

Chapter 18
Finding Your Target Audience
The Parable of the Sower

Introduction: Understanding Your Audience

In the vast landscape of business, identifying and engaging with your target audience is paramount for success. The Parable of the Sower, shared by Jesus in the Gospels, provides profound insights into this process, illustrating the importance of understanding the receptivity of different hearts to the message being shared. In this chapter, we delve into the Parable of the Sower and uncover its applications in the context of business, particularly in finding and connecting with our target audience effectively.

The Parable of the Sower: Insights into Audience Engagement

The Parable of the Sower recounts a Sower scattering seeds onto various types of soil, each representing different conditions of the human heart. Some seeds fell on the path, others on rocky ground, some among thorns, and yet others on fertile soil, each yielding different outcomes.

Understanding the Soil: Translating to Audience Segmentation

Just as the different types of soil represent varying receptivity to the seeds, businesses must segment their audience based on factors such as demographics, psychographics, and behaviors. By understanding the characteristics and preferences of different audience segments, businesses can tailor their marketing efforts to resonate more effectively with each group.

Application in Business: Tailoring Your Approach

1. **Segmentation and Targeting:** Segment your audience based on key criteria such as age, gender, interests, and purchasing behavior. By understanding the unique needs and preferences of each segment, you can tailor your messaging and marketing strategies to resonate more effectively with your target audience.

2. **Personalized Marketing**: Utilize personalized marketing techniques such as email segmentation, targeted advertising, and personalized content to engage with your audience on a more individual level. By delivering relevant and personalized messages, you can capture the attention and interest of your target audience more effectively.

3. **Market Research:** Invest in market research to gain insights into the needs, preferences, and pain points of your target audience. By understanding the motivations and challenges faced by your audience, you can develop products, services, and marketing campaigns that address their specific needs and offer meaningful solutions.

4. **Feedback and Iteration:** Solicit feedback from your audience through surveys, focus groups, and social media channels. Use this feedback to iterate and refine your products, services, and marketing strategies to better meet the needs and expectations of your target audience over time.

Conclusion: Nurturing Connections with Your Audience

In conclusion, the Parable of the Sower offers timeless wisdom on the importance of understanding and engaging with your target audience effectively. By segmenting your audience, personalizing your marketing efforts, conducting market research, and soliciting feedback, you can cultivate meaningful connections with your target audience and position your business for success in today's competitive marketplace. As Christian entrepreneurs, let us embrace the principles of audience engagement found in this parable, recognizing that every interaction with our audience is an opportunity to sow seeds of trust, loyalty, and connection that will yield a bountiful harvest of success in the future.

Chapter 19
Finding Your Niche
The Call of Moses

Introduction: Discovering Your Unique Path

In the vast landscape of business, finding your niche is essential for standing out in a crowded marketplace and establishing a distinctive presence. The Call of Moses provides profound insights into the process of discovering and embracing one's unique calling or niche. In this chapter, we explore the story of Moses and uncover its applications in the context of business, particularly in identifying and capitalizing on your unique strengths, passions, and areas of expertise.

The Call of Moses: Unveiling Your Unique Calling

The story of Moses begins with a humble shepherd tending his flock in the wilderness when he encounters a burning bush that is not consumed by the flames. Through this extraordinary encounter, God calls Moses to lead the Israelites out of slavery in Egypt, setting him on a path of purpose and significance.

Embracing Your Unique Calling: Translating to Business

Just as Moses was called to a specific task and mission, each of us has unique gifts, talents, and experiences that shape our individual paths in business. Embracing our calling or niche requires self-awareness, courage, and a willingness to step into the unknown.

Application in Business: Carving Your Niche

1. **Identify Your Strengths and Passions**: Reflect on your strengths, passions, and areas of expertise. What are you uniquely good at? What activities bring you joy and fulfillment? Identifying these core attributes will help you uncover potential niches where you can excel and make a meaningful impact.

2. **Research Market Opportunities**: Conduct market research to identify gaps, opportunities, and underserved needs in your industry or niche. Explore emerging trends, competitor offerings, and customer preferences to uncover areas where your unique skills and perspectives can add value.

3. **Test and Validate Your Ideas**: Test and validate your niche ideas through experimentation and feedback. Launch pilot projects, conduct surveys, or offer prototype products or services to gauge interest and gather insights from potential customers. Use this feedback to refine and iterate your niche concept.

4. **Establish Your Unique Positioning**: Define your unique positioning within your chosen niche. What sets you apart

from competitors? What value do you offer that others cannot replicate? Clearly articulating your unique selling proposition (USP) will help you attract and resonate with your target audience.

Conclusion: Thriving in Your Niche

In conclusion, the story of Moses reminds us of the importance of discovering and embracing our unique calling or niche in business. By identifying our strengths, passions, and areas of expertise, conducting market research, testing and validating our ideas, and establishing our unique positioning, we can carve out a distinctive path to success and fulfillment. As Christian entrepreneurs, let us heed the call to stewardship and excellence, using our businesses as vehicles for impact and transformation in the world. In finding and thriving in our niche, we honor God's plan for our lives and fulfill our potential to make a difference in the lives of others.

Chapter 20
Continuous Improvement:
The Growth of the Early Church

Introduction: The Path to Sustainable Growth

The early church experienced remarkable growth and expansion in the face of adversity, laying the foundation for Christianity to become a global movement. Central to this growth was the principle of continuous improvement—an ongoing commitment to learning, adapting, and evolving in response to changing circumstances. In this final chapter, we'll explore how the growth of the early church exemplifies the importance of continuous improvement in sustaining and expanding your business.

1. **Embracing Change**: The early church faced constant change and opposition, yet it remained resilient and adaptable. Similarly, businesses must embrace change as a constant in today's dynamic marketplace. Continuously monitor industry trends, consumer behavior, and technological advancements, then adapt your strategies and offerings accordingly to stay relevant and competitive.

2. **Learning from Feedback: Listening to the Voice of the Customer**: The early church valued feedback and input from its members, allowing it to address emerging needs and challenges effectively. Likewise, businesses must listen to the voice of the customer, gathering feedback through surveys, reviews, and customer interactions. Use this

feedback to identify areas for improvement and innovation, driving customer satisfaction and loyalty.

3. **Experimentation and Innovation: Trying New Approaches**: The early church was not afraid to experiment with new methods and approaches to ministry, leading to innovative practices and strategies. Similarly, businesses must foster a culture of experimentation and innovation, encouraging employees to explore new ideas and take calculated risks. Embrace a mindset of continuous learning and improvement, iterating on processes and products to drive growth and innovation.

4. **Building on Successes: Scaling and Expanding Wisely**: As the early church experienced growth and success, it remained grounded in its mission and values, ensuring that expansion was purposeful and sustainable. Similarly, businesses must scale and expand wisely, building on their successes while maintaining focus on their core values and objectives. Avoid the pitfalls of rapid expansion without a solid foundation, prioritizing long-term sustainability over short-term gains.

Conclusion: The Journey of Growth and Transformation

In conclusion, the growth of the early church serves as a powerful example of the transformative power of continuous improvement. By embracing change, learning from feedback, experimenting with new ideas, and scaling wisely, businesses can sustainably grow and thrive in today's competitive landscape. As Christian entrepreneurs, let us heed the lessons of the early church and commit ourselves to a journey of continuous improvement, always striving to better serve our customers, employees, and communities. In doing so, we honor God's call to stewardship and excellence, using our businesses as vehicles for positive change and impact in the world.

Made in the USA
Columbia, SC
24 May 2024